Fun Fan Facts:
The Unofficial NBA Edition

Charlotte Hornets

Everything Young Hornets Fans Should Know

By: Jake Liam

Dedication

To every Hornets fan who stuck through the ups, downs, and everything in between. The buzz never left.

THE NBA BY THE NUMBERS

MOST NBA CHAMPIONSHIPS*

- CELTICS (18) †
- LAKERS (17)
- WARRIORS (7)
- BULLS (6)
- SPURS (5)

As of the 2024-25 Season. † One Trophy = 4 Championships.

NBA HISTORY SNAPSHOT

1946 — NBA Founded
1954 — Shot Clock Introduced
1979 — 3-Point Line Added
2023 — NBA Cup Introduced

BIG NUMBERS

$156 million
Stephen Curry's est. earnings in the 24-25 season

7'7"
Tallest player in NBA history (Gheorghe Mureșan & Manute Bol)

30 | 4 | 82

30 — Teams Competing in the NBA
4 — Playoff Rounds
82 — Games Per Season

CHARLOTTE HORNETS
IN THE NBA

- FOUNDED: 1988 †
- NBA TITLES: 0
- CONFERENCE TITLES: 0*

38 Seasons in the NBA

*† Founding dates are complicated & may cause arguments at Thanksgiving. Ask someone born before color TV. All Titles reflect pre-relocation franchise history. * As of 2024-25 Season.*

NBA ALL-TIME MVP LEADERS

KAREEM ABDUL-JABBAR (6) ★ MICHAEL JORDAN (5) ★ BILL RUSSELL (5)

EASTERN CONFERENCE

- Atlantic – **Celtics**
- Atlantic – **Nets**
- Atlantic – **Knicks**
- Atlantic – **76ers**
- Atlantic – **Raptors**
- Central – **Bulls**
- Central – **Cavaliers**
- Central – **Pistons**
- Central – **Pacers**
- Central – **Bucks**
- Southeast – **Hawks**
- Southeast – **Hornets**
- Southeast – **Heat**
- Southeast – **Magic**
- Southeast – **Wizards**

WESTERN CONFERENCE

- Pacific – **Lakers**
- Pacific – **Clippers**
- Pacific – **Warriors**
- Pacific – **Suns**
- Pacific – **Kings**
- Northwest – **Nuggets**
- Northwest – **Timberwolves**
- Northwest – **Thunder**
- Northwest – **Trail Blazers**
- Northwest – **Jazz**
- Southwest – **Mavericks**
- Southwest – **Rockets**
- Southwest – **Spurs**
- Southwest – **Pelicans**
- Southwest – **Grizzlies**

Introduction

Welcome, fans! Whether you're new to cheering for the Charlotte Hornets or you've been bleeding the team colors your whole life, this book is packed with fun, exciting facts about your favorite team. Get ready to impress your friends and family with everything you know about the Hornets.

Quick Timeout

This book is packed with stats. Like, A LOT of stats. Every fact was checked, double-checked, and triple-checked. But here's the thing about basketball history: not everyone agrees on everything. Ask someone who watched games before color TV and someone who grew up with instant replay and you'll get two completely different answers. My dad, stepdad, uncle, and grandpa all argued about the same fact. Four people. Four answers. All of them think they're right. So if you spot something that doesn't match what you've heard, congratulations. You might be a bigger fan than the people who helped make this book. And honestly? That's pretty cool.

HOW IT WORKS

THE SEASON

82 Games. One Goal.

Each team plays 82 games.
Win enough to make the
Playoffs.
Every game counts!

PLAYOFFS

30 Teams. 16 Make It.

8 per conference make the playoffs.
Win=Advance | Lose=Go Home
Best record
gets home court!

PLAYOFF ROUNDS

Best of 7. Win 4 or Go Home.

4 rounds of pure pressure.
Every series is do-or-die!

OVERTIME?

5 More Minutes.

Keep playing until
someone pulls ahead.
No ties. Ever.

THE FINALS

One Series. One Champion.

Winner lifts the Trophy.
Legend status unlocked.

How the NBA Works

At first glance, basketball feels simple. Ten players. One ball. Two hoops. Go.

Then the NBA adds the layers.

An 82-game regular season. A draft where bad teams pick first. Playoffs that last two full months. Superstars who can change everything with one trade. Dynasties that rise, fall, and rise again.

And somehow, it all works.

The NBA is built on one big idea: every team gets a chance to reset, reload, and rise again. No relegation. No dropping down to a lower league. Just basketball, every night, from October through June.

It is a league designed for drama, stars, and comebacks. And once you understand the flow, it is impossible to stop watching.

The League Setup

The NBA has 30 teams, spread across the United States and Canada. Those teams are split into two conferences:

- Eastern Conference
- Western Conference

Each conference has three divisions, mostly based on geography. Divisions matter for scheduling, but not as much as they used to.

Every team plays 82 regular season games, usually from October through April. Home games. Road games. Back-to-back nights. Long road trips. The season is a marathon before the sprint even starts.

Win games, and you climb the standings. Lose too many, and the pressure builds fast.

How Games Are Played

An NBA game has four quarters, each lasting 12 minutes. That means 48 minutes of game time, plus timeouts, free throws, and the occasional coach argument that adds another 20 minutes nobody planned for.

Scoring is simple:

- A shot inside the three-point line is worth 2 points
- A shot beyond the arc is worth 3 points
- Free throws are worth 1 point

If the score is tied at the end of regulation, the game goes to overtime, which lasts 5 minutes. Still tied? Another overtime. Keep going until someone wins.

There is a shot clock too. Teams have 24 seconds to take a shot. No standing around. No holding the ball forever. Keep it moving.

The Regular Season Race

The regular season is long for a reason. It tests everything.

Depth. Health. Focus. Patience.

Teams play opponents from both conferences, but they face conference rivals more often. By the end of the season, each conference's top teams have earned their playoff spots the hard way.

The goal is simple: make the playoffs. But there is a twist.

The NBA Cup

In 2023, the NBA added something new to the middle of the season. Something with actual stakes. They called it the In-Season Tournament, now known as the NBA Cup.

It works like this: Every team plays a small group stage during November and December, with special court designs that look like nothing else in basketball. The best teams advance to a knockout round held in Las Vegas.

The winners split a prize pool. Players earn bonus money. And for the first time, a team could lift a trophy before the playoffs even started.

Some fans are still warming up to it. Some players love it. But the moment a team starts treating it seriously and a crowd shows up buzzing in December, it feels like something.

Which, honestly, sounds about right.

The Play-In Tournament

Instead of sending the top eight teams from each conference straight to the playoffs, the NBA added something new. The Play-In Tournament.

Here is how it works:

- Teams ranked 1 through 6 in each conference are safe
- Teams ranked 7 through 10 fight for the final two playoff spots

The 7 and 8 seeds have an advantage. Win once and you are in. Lose and you still get one more shot. The 9 and 10 seeds have to win twice in a row just to earn a first-round matchup.

It turns the end of the season into a sprint. Every game suddenly matters more. Fans love it. Coaches age rapidly.

The NBA Playoffs

Once the playoffs begin, everything tightens.

Sixteen teams enter. Eight from each conference. Every round is a best-of-seven games series. That means the first team to win four games moves on:

- First Round
- Conference Semifinals
- Conference Finals
- NBA Finals

Home-court advantage matters. Crowds get louder. Rotations get shorter. Superstars play heavier minutes. One bad quarter can flip a series. One great performance can define a career.

By the time the NBA Finals arrive in June, only two teams are left. One from the East. One from the West. Four wins away from a championship. Four wins away from history.

The NBA Draft: Hope Begins Here

Here is where the NBA gets clever. Every summer, new players enter the league through the NBA Draft. Teams take turns selecting college players, international stars, and teenagers straight out of high school.

The teams that finished with the worst records get the best odds to pick early through the Draft Lottery. It is not guaranteed, but it gives struggling franchises a real shot at changing their future with one pick.

That means one bad season does not doom you forever. It might actually change everything. Some franchises are rebuilt by a single draft night moment.

Hope shows up wearing a new jersey.

No Relegation. All Pressure.

Unlike many global sports leagues, NBA teams never drop down to a lower league. They always stay in the NBA.

That does not mean there is no pressure.

Fans remember losing seasons. Owners make changes. Coaches get replaced. Players get traded. Every year is a test of direction, patience, and belief.

Stars, Systems, and Showtime

The NBA is famous for its stars. But stars do not win alone.

Teams need chemistry. Coaches need systems. Role players need to deliver on the biggest stages. One injury. One hot streak. One trade deadline deal. Any of it can flip a season.

That balance between individual brilliance and team basketball is what makes the league special.

Fast breaks. Buzzer-beaters. Game 7s. And moments that get replayed forever. That is the NBA.

Once you get the flow, it is pure electricity.

Charlotte Hornets Facts

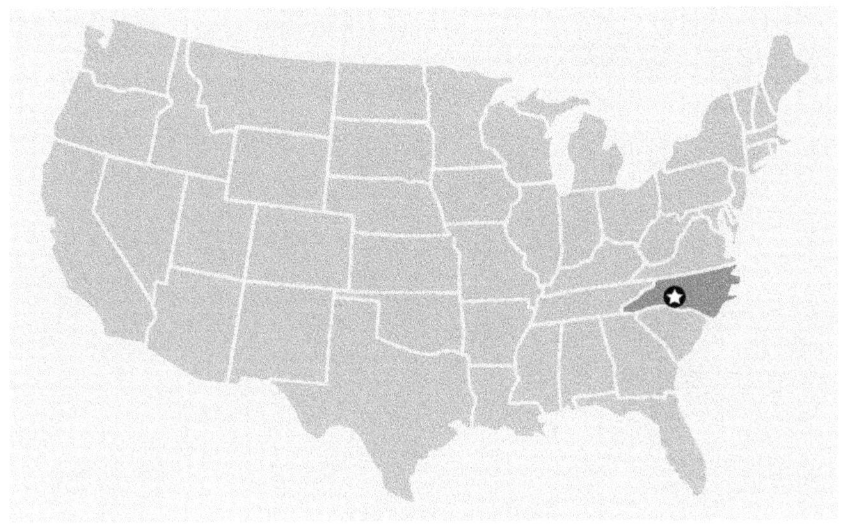

Home City

Charlotte, North Carolina

Metro Area Population

About 2.8 Million

Home Arena

Spectrum Center

Arena Capacity

19,077

Conference / Division

Eastern Conference / Southeast Division

Famous Local Food

BBQ pork, hushpuppies, sweet potato pie, boiled peanuts

Chapter 1: Where the Buzz Began

1. Why "Hornets"? A Name with a Sting

The Charlotte Hornets did not just pick a random insect and call it a day. This name goes all the way back to the American Revolutionary War, which is not where you expect a basketball story to start. When British General Cornwallis rolled into Charlotte in 1780, he got a very rude welcome from the locals, who fought back so aggressively that he called the city "a hornet's nest of rebellion."

That line stuck around for over 200 years, which is honestly impressive for something a frustrated general said after getting annoyed. The nickname became part of Charlotte's identity. It meant the people were tough, loud, and not interested in backing down, even when the odds were not in their favor. Basically, the kind of attitude every sports team wishes it could bottle and sell.

So when the NBA gave Charlotte a team in the 1980s, "Hornets" was the perfect choice. It sounds cool, it has history, and it comes with built-in energy. Plus, if you have ever actually been near a hornet, you know they are fast, aggressive, and very annoying to deal with. That is exactly the vibe you want your opponents thinking about.

2. Born in 1988: Charlotte Gets in the Game

In 1988, Charlotte officially joined the NBA, which was a huge deal for a city that already loved basketball. North Carolina was basically obsessed with college hoops, but now it had a professional team to cheer for. The Hornets were part of the league's expansion, and the city wasted no time jumping on board.

Their first game came on November 4, 1988, against the Cleveland Cavaliers. They lost, which is pretty normal for a brand new team that is still figuring out who can actually dribble under pressure. But nobody in Charlotte cared about the scoreboard that much. The building was packed, the crowd was loud, and the message was clear that this city was ready for the NBA.

Starting from scratch is never easy. You do not get superstars handed to you, and you definitely do not start winning right away. The Hornets had to build everything from the ground up, from players to identity to confidence. The one thing they did not have to build was fan support, because Charlotte showed up immediately and made sure everyone knew this team mattered.

3. The Teal Takeover: How the Hornets Became Cool Overnight

When the Hornets picked teal and purple as their team colors, it probably felt like a gamble. Most teams at the time played it safe with classic colors, but Charlotte went in a completely different direction. Teal was bold, different, and honestly kind of weird if you were used to traditional sports uniforms.

Then something unexpected happened. Everyone decided it was awesome.

In the early 1990s, Hornets gear exploded across the country. People who had never watched a full basketball game were suddenly wearing teal jackets and snapback hats. It became one of the biggest trends in sports fashion. Celebrities wore it, kids wore it, and entire schools looked like unofficial Hornets fan clubs even if they lived nowhere near North Carolina.

The Hornets did not just create a team, they created a style. They proved that looking different could actually make you more popular, not less. Even today, those classic jerseys are still considered some of the best ever made, which is wild when you remember it all started with a color choice that could have gone very wrong.

4. The Charlotte Coliseum: Loud, Huge, and Kind of Intimidating

The Charlotte Coliseum opened in 1988, and it was massive. Nearly 24,000 seats, making it the largest basketball-specific arena in NBA history at the time. Some people thought it was too big. How was a brand new team in a mid-sized Southern city going to fill all those seats?

Turns out that was not a problem.

The Hornets led the NBA in attendance in eight of their first nine seasons. Not eighth in attendance. First. More fans showed up to watch the Hornets than the Knicks, the Lakers, or the Bulls. Charlotte even set an NBA record by drawing over one million fans in their very first year.

Then came the sellout streak. Starting in late 1988, the Hornets sold out 371 consecutive games. Nearly nine straight seasons of packed houses. Every seat filled. Every game night. The arena earned its nickname, The

Hive, not because of some special design trick, but because 24,000 fans kept showing up and making noise together.

For visiting teams, that was the problem. Playing in Charlotte meant facing the biggest crowd in the league, game after game, with no relief in sight.

5. When the Team Left: The Day Charlotte Lost the Hornets

In 2002, something happened that every sports fan secretly fears. The Hornets left Charlotte and moved to New Orleans. After years of tension between the team's owner and the city, the decision was made, and just like that, the team was gone.

For fans, it felt terrible. Imagine growing up with a team, going to games, wearing the colors, knowing the players, and then suddenly they are not yours anymore. Same name, same history, just in a different city. It felt like someone hit pause on basketball in Charlotte and forgot to press play again.

The NBA did eventually give Charlotte a new team, the Bobcats, but it did not feel the same at first. The original Hornets had built something special, and that kind of connection does not just reset overnight. The good news is that this story does not end there, because Charlotte was not done fighting to get its identity back. We will get to that later.

6. Muggsy Bogues: The 5'3" Giant (1988-1997)

Tyrone "Muggsy" Bogues was the shortest player in NBA history at 5 feet 3 inches tall, which is about the height of some middle schoolers. That alone sounds impossible when you remember he was playing against guys pushing 7 feet tall. Most people would look at that height difference and say there is no way this works, but Muggsy did not just survive in the NBA. He thrived.

What made him special was not size, it was speed, toughness, and confidence. Muggsy was lightning fast, could steal the ball from anyone, and had zero fear. Imagine trying to dribble while someone half your size is zipping around your knees like a blur and taking the ball before you even realize it is gone. That was Muggsy every night. He also became one of the best passers in the league, running the offense like a coach on the court.

Fans loved him because he felt relatable and unbelievable at the same time. He proved that heart and skill could beat size, which is basically every kid's dream when they step onto a court. Muggsy did not just play for the Hornets. He became one of the most iconic players in franchise history and a symbol of what makes basketball fun.

Muggsy Bogues racing up the court during his college days in 1985. At just 5-foot-3, he was the shortest player in NBA history. But quick feet, fearless defense, and lightning passes soon made him a Charlotte Hornets legend. Proof that heart and hustle can beat height any day. *Photo: Tyrone "Muggsy" Bogues, 1985. Duke Chronicle photograph. Public domain. Source: Wikimedia Commons.*

7. Larry Johnson: The Superstar with an Alter Ego (1991-1996)

Larry Johnson arrived in Charlotte in 1991 and immediately became a star. He was the number one overall pick in the draft, which means the Hornets were expecting something big. What they got was a powerful forward who could score, rebound, and play with the kind of energy that made fans jump out of their seats.

But Larry Johnson was not just known for his game. He had one of the most famous commercials in basketball history, where he dressed up as an old woman named "Grandmama" and still somehow dominated on the court. It was funny, weird, and completely unforgettable. Suddenly, he was not just a player. He was a character that everyone knew.

On the court, he helped turn the Hornets into a real threat in the Eastern Conference. He played with strength, confidence, and a little bit of swagger that matched the team's growing identity. For a few years, he was the face of the franchise and one of the main reasons Charlotte became one of the more exciting teams to watch.

8. Alonzo Mourning: Power, Passion, and Intensity (1992-1995)

Alonzo Mourning joined the Hornets in 1992 and brought something every team needs but cannot always find. He brought attitude. From the moment he stepped on the court, it was clear he was not there to be nice. He was there to dominate.

Mourning was a force in the paint. He blocked shots, grabbed rebounds, and made life miserable for anyone who tried to score near the basket. On offense, he could score with power and confidence, and on defense, he made opponents think twice before even entering the lane. He played like every possession mattered, which made him one of the most intense players in the league.

The combination of Mourning and Larry Johnson gave the Hornets a young, exciting core that fans believed could take them deep into the playoffs. They were strong, talented, and fearless. For a while, it looked like Charlotte had found the perfect duo to build around.

9. Kemba Walker: The Heart of Charlotte Basketball (2011-2019)

Kemba Walker did not arrive with as much hype as some of the earlier stars, but he quickly became the player Charlotte fans connected with the most. Drafted in 2011, he worked his way into becoming the leader of the team through skill, effort, and consistency.

Kemba was not the biggest player on the court, but he played like he had something to prove every night. He could score from anywhere, hit big shots in clutch moments, and carry the offense when the team needed it most. When games got close, everyone in the building knew who was getting the ball, and somehow, he still found a way to deliver.

What made Kemba special was the way he embraced the city. He stayed loyal during tough seasons, gave everything he had on the court, and became the face of the franchise during the Hornets' rebuilding years. Even without championships, he earned something just as important in Charlotte. Respect.

10. LaMelo Ball: The New Face of Buzz City (2020-Present)

LaMelo Ball entered the NBA in 2020 with a lot of attention already on him. He had been famous for years before he even played a professional game, which meant expectations were sky high. Some people wondered if he could actually live up to the hype once he reached the NBA.

It did not take long to get an answer. LaMelo brought a completely different style to the Hornets. Flashy passes, deep three-pointers, and a creativity that made every game feel unpredictable. He plays with confidence and imagination, which makes him one of the most entertaining players to watch in the league.

More importantly, he gave Hornets fans something they had been waiting for. Hope. With LaMelo leading the team, there is a real belief that Charlotte can build something exciting again. He represents the future of the franchise, and if things go right, the buzz in Buzz City could get louder than ever.

11. The 1993 Playoff Buzzer-Beater: Charlotte Goes Crazy

In 1993, the Hornets made the playoffs for the first time in franchise history, which already felt like a huge win for a young team. They faced the Boston Celtics in the first round, and most people expected the experienced Celtics to handle business. Instead, Charlotte turned the series into a full-on battle.

Game 4 became the moment everyone remembers. With the game on the line and the Hornets needing a win to take the series, Alonzo Mourning got the ball near the basket. The clock was ticking down, the crowd was on its feet, and everything felt like it was moving in slow motion. Mourning turned, put up a short shot, and the ball dropped through the net right as time expired.

The arena exploded. Fans were jumping, screaming, and probably losing their voices all at once. That shot did not just win the game, it won the series and gave Charlotte its first playoff victory ever. For a franchise that was still figuring itself out, that moment felt like a message. The Hornets had arrived, and they were not just here to participate.

12. The Kobe Trade: The Real "What If" Moment

Charlotte fans sometimes bring up missing Shaquille O'Neal in 1992. The Hornets had the second pick that year, just one spot behind Orlando, who took Shaq first overall. Close call, but they never actually had him.

The Kobe Bryant situation? That one hurts more, because they did have him.

In the 1996 NBA Draft, the Hornets selected a 17-year-old guard named Kobe Bryant with the 13th pick. He was coming straight out of high school, which was rare back then and made some teams nervous. Charlotte's head coach reportedly said the team had no use for him. So they traded him to the Los Angeles Lakers for center Vlade Divac.

The trade almost fell apart when Divac threatened to retire rather than move to Charlotte. But eventually he agreed, the deal went through, and Kobe became a Laker.

Five championships later, everyone knew exactly what Charlotte had given away. Kobe became one of the greatest players in NBA history, and he did it all wearing purple and gold instead of teal and purple. Fans still wonder what could have been if the Hornets had just kept the 17-year-old kid with the ridiculous work ethic and zero fear.

13. Mourning vs. Johnson: When Teammates Became Rivals

For a while, Larry Johnson and Alonzo Mourning looked like the perfect duo. One was powerful and flashy, the other was intense and dominant, and together they gave the Hornets a real chance to compete. Then things started to fall apart.

The two stars began clashing behind the scenes. Different personalities, different styles, and a growing tension that the team could not ignore. It was the kind of situation where everyone could tell something was wrong, even if nobody said it out loud at first. Eventually, the Hornets had to make a decision.

That decision led to both players being traded, and just like that, one of the most exciting young duos in the league was gone. Instead of building a long-term contender, Charlotte had to reset again. It was a reminder that talent alone is not enough. Chemistry matters, and when it breaks, everything can fall apart faster than expected.

14. The Bobcats Era: Starting Over... Again

After the Hornets left in 2002, Charlotte spent two years without an NBA team before the league returned with a new franchise in 2004. This team was called the Bobcats, and while it brought basketball back to the city, it did not feel the same.

The Bobcats struggled almost immediately. Wins were hard to find, stars were harder to keep, and the team never quite built the same identity the Hornets had in the 1990s. Fans showed up, but the excitement was different. It felt more like hope than confidence.

Starting over is always tough, especially when people are still remembering what came before. The Bobcats were trying to create something new while living in the shadow of the old Hornets. It took time, patience, and a lot of losing seasons before things started to change.

15. The Worst Season Ever: 7 Wins, 59 Losses

The 2011-2012 season is one Charlotte fans would probably like to forget, but it is also impossible to ignore. The Bobcats finished with a record of 7 wins and 59 losses, which is the worst winning percentage in NBA history.

To put that into perspective, they lost so many games that winning felt like a rare event. Fans would come to games hoping for a surprise, and most nights, they got a reminder of just how tough rebuilding can be. It was frustrating, exhausting, and honestly a little painful to watch.

But even seasons like that matter. They show how hard it is to build a team from the ground up and how much things can change over time. The same franchise that once struggled to win games would eventually bring the Hornets name back and start building something new again. Sometimes the lowest points end up being part of the comeback story.

16. Teal Took Over the World: The Coolest Color Ever

In the early 1990s, the Charlotte Hornets did something no one saw coming. They accidentally became the coolest team in sports, and it had a lot to do with one color. Teal. Not red. Not blue. Teal. A color that most teams probably would have laughed at suddenly became the hottest thing in the country.

Hornets gear was everywhere. Jackets, hats, shirts, starter coats that somehow made you feel like a celebrity just for putting one on. Kids who had never watched a Hornets game were walking around dressed head to toe in teal and purple like they had season tickets. Even celebrities jumped on the trend, which made it spread even faster.

The funniest part is that it did not even matter if the team won or lost. The Hornets had already won the fashion championship. To this day, their classic gear is still considered some of the best ever, which proves that sometimes looking cool is almost as powerful as actually winning games.

17. Hugo the Hornet: The Mascot with No Fear

Every team has a mascot, but not every mascot is flying through the air like a superhero. Hugo the Hornet is not just someone in a costume waving at the crowd. Hugo dunks, flips, dances, and occasionally does things that make you wonder if someone forgot to tell him gravity exists.

Hugo became famous for his crazy stunts during games. We are talking trampoline dunks, backflips, and moments where he launches himself into the air like he is trying out for an action movie. At one point, he even rappelled down from the ceiling, which is either awesome or slightly terrifying depending on how much you trust the ropes.

Mascots are supposed to entertain the crowd, but Hugo took that job very seriously. He turned halftime into a full show and gave fans something to talk about even when the team was not winning. If nothing else, you knew you were going to see something wild when Hugo was in the building.

18. The Name Came Back: The Comeback Nobody Saw Coming

In 2013, New Orleans made a surprising announcement. They were rebranding to the Pelicans, a name more connected to Louisiana's identity. That meant the Hornets name was suddenly available again.

Charlotte moved fast. Team owner Michael Jordan (yes, that Michael Jordan, we will get to that story in Chapter 5) worked with the NBA to reclaim everything: the name, the colors, and the original franchise history from 1988 to 2002. All those Muggsy Bogues memories, the Grandmama commercials, the sold-out Hive, it officially belonged to Charlotte again.

On May 20, 2014, the Bobcats became the Charlotte Hornets. The teal and purple returned. The logo came back. And fans who had waited twelve years finally got to cheer for their real team again. Not many cities get a second chance at their basketball identity, but Charlotte grabbed it the moment the door opened.

19. Buzz City Energy: Fans Who Never Quit

Charlotte might not be the biggest market in the NBA, but its fans show up like it is Game 7 every night. The nickname "Buzz City" is not just something that sounds cool. It actually describes the energy inside the arena when things are going right.

Even during tough seasons, fans stuck with the team. That says a lot, because sticking with a team through losing seasons is not exactly easy. It takes patience, loyalty, and a little bit of stubbornness. Charlotte fans have all three.

When the team starts winning, that energy gets even louder. The arena fills up, the crowd gets into every play, and suddenly it feels like the old Coliseum days again. Buzz City is not just a nickname. It is a reminder that this fan base has always been ready to explode when the moment is right.

20. Jerseys, Courts, and Some Questionable Choices

The Hornets have had some of the best jerseys in NBA history. They have also had a few that probably made fans stare at them for a second and go, "Wait... what is that?" That is part of the fun when a team is willing to try new things.

The classic teal and purple look is still the gold standard. Clean, bold, and instantly recognizable. But over the years, there have been alternate jerseys, special editions, and designs that felt like someone got a little too creative late at night. Some worked. Some definitely did not.

The court designs have also changed over time, with bright colors and patterns that make Hornets games stand out on TV. Whether you love every design or not, one thing is clear. The Hornets are never boring when it comes to style. They would rather take a risk than blend in, and honestly, that fits their whole identity.

Chapter 5: Today & The Future of the Hive

21. Spectrum Center: A New Home for Buzz City

The Hornets currently play at the Spectrum Center, which opened in 2005 when the team was still known as the Bobcats. Located in downtown Charlotte, the arena gave the franchise a fresh start after the difficult years of losing the original Hornets and rebuilding from scratch. It is smaller than the old Coliseum, but it feels more modern, louder, and much more connected to the city.

Over time, the arena has been upgraded with new technology, better seating, and a game-day experience designed to keep fans engaged from start to finish. The location also helps, since being right in the middle of the city makes it easy for fans to show up, hang out, and turn games into full events instead of just something you attend and leave.

When the Hornets name returned in 2014, the Spectrum Center finally started to feel like a true home again. The colors were back, the identity made sense, and the energy inside the building began to grow. It may not be the biggest arena in the league, but when it gets loud, it still carries that classic Charlotte buzz.

22. Building Around LaMelo: The New Core

LaMelo Ball was drafted third overall in 2020, and it did not take long for him to change the direction of the franchise. He won Rookie of the Year in 2021, which immediately put the Hornets back on the map as a team people actually wanted to watch again. His style is fast, creative, and sometimes completely unpredictable in the best way possible.

The Hornets have been working to build a team around him, adding young players and trying to develop a core that can grow together. Players like Miles Bridges and others have shown flashes of talent, giving fans hope that this is not just another rebuild that goes nowhere. The challenge has been consistency, because potential only matters if it turns into wins.

Still, having a player like LaMelo changes everything. He draws attention, creates highlights, and makes teammates better when things are clicking. If the front office can put the right pieces around him, Charlotte has a real chance to turn excitement into something much bigger.

23. The Michael Jordan Era: Ownership Matters

Remember when the Hornets got their name back in 2014? You can thank Michael Jordan for that.

In 2010, Michael Jordan became the majority owner of the Charlotte franchise, making him the first former NBA player to own a team outright. That alone made Charlotte one of the most interesting teams in the league, because having one of the greatest players of all time in charge is not something most teams can say.

Jordan made reclaiming the Hornets name a priority. He understood that Charlotte fans never stopped missing the original team, and bringing back the name, the colors, and the history was not just nostalgia, it was good business. When the Pelicans rebrand opened the door in 2013, Jordan walked through it.

Building a winner? That has been tougher. His teams made the playoffs just twice and never got past the first round. Proof that even the greatest player ever cannot just will a franchise to success from the owner's box.

In 2023, Jordan sold his majority stake in the team but remained connected to the franchise as a minority owner. His time in charge helped stabilize the organization and restore its identity, even if the championships never came. His impact is still part of the team's story, especially when it comes to bringing the Hornets name back to life.

24. Can the Hornets Compete Again?

The Hornets have had moments of excitement over the years, but they are still searching for consistent success. Making the playoffs is one thing. Becoming a real contender is something completely different. That is the challenge the team is facing right now.

The Eastern Conference is stacked with strong teams, which makes the path even tougher. Charlotte needs development, smart decisions, and a little bit of luck to move up the standings. Injuries, roster moves, and coaching all play a role, and one mistake can set a team back quickly.

The good news is that rebuilds can turn around faster than people expect in the NBA. One great draft pick, one smart trade, or one breakout season can change everything. The Hornets are not there yet, but they are in a position where things could start moving in the right direction.

25. Why Fans Still Believe in Buzz City

Being a Hornets fan has not always been easy. There have been losing seasons, tough decisions, and moments where it felt like progress was moving slower than expected. But through all of it, the fan base has stayed loyal, which says a lot about the connection between the team and the city.

There is something about the Hornets that keeps people believing. Maybe it is the history, maybe it is the colors, or maybe it is the feeling that something exciting could happen at any moment. When the team starts playing well, the energy comes back quickly, and it reminds everyone what Charlotte basketball can feel like.

The future is not guaranteed, but the foundation is there. A young star, a strong identity, and a fan base that refuses to give up. That combination has worked before in the NBA, and if it comes together again, Buzz City could be louder than ever.

Bonus Trivia Quiz!

You think you are a true Hornets fan? Try this bonus quiz!

1. Why is Charlotte called the "Hornets"?

A) A famous insect in the area

B) A Revolutionary War nickname

C) A college mascot

D) A random team vote

2. What year did the Hornets first join the NBA?

A) 1985

B) 1988

C) 1990

D) 1992

3. What colors made the Hornets famous in the 1990s?

A) Red and black

B) Blue and white

C) Teal and purple

D) Green and gold

4. How many consecutive games did the Hornets sell out at the Charlotte Coliseum?

A) 50 games

B) 150 games

C) 371 games

D) 500 games

5. What happened to the Hornets in 2002?

A) They won a championship

B) They changed colors

C) They moved to New Orleans

D) They merged with another team

6. How tall was Muggsy Bogues?

A) 5'8"

B) 6'0"

C) 5'3"

D) 6'5"

7. What nickname did Larry Johnson use in commercials?

A) Big LJ

B) Grandmama

C) The King

D) The Machine

8. What position did Alonzo Mourning dominate?

A) Point guard

B) Shooting guard

C) Center

D) Small forward

9. Which Hornets player became the face of the team in the 2010s?

A) LaMelo Ball

B) Kemba Walker

C) Dell Curry

D) Glen Rice

10. What major award did LaMelo Ball win in 2021?

A) MVP

B) Rookie of the Year

C) Defensive Player of the Year

D) Sixth Man of the Year

11. What famous moment happened in the 1993 playoffs?

A) A missed dunk

B) A buzzer-beater by Alonzo Mourning

C) A triple overtime game

D) A fan ran on the court

12. Who did the Hornets draft in 1996 but trade away?

A) Michael Jordan

B) Kobe Bryant

C) Shaquille O'Neal

D) Tim Duncan

13. What was Charlotte's team name before returning to the Hornets?

A) Cougars

B) Bobcats

C) Panthers

D) Kings

14. Who became majority owner of the team in 2010?

A) Magic Johnson

B) LeBron James

C) Michael Jordan

D) Larry Bird

15. What is the name of the Hornets' current arena?

A) Charlotte Dome

B) Buzz Arena

C) Spectrum Center

D) Hive Stadium

Super Fan Secret Challenge

Only a true Hornets fan will know this.

(No Answer Provided)

What was the name of Charlotte's original NBA arena before the Spectrum Center?

A) Queen City Arena

B) Charlotte Coliseum

C) Carolina Dome

D) Hornets Hall

Answer Key

1. B) A Revolutionary War nickname

2. B) 1988

3. C) Teal and purple

4. C) 371 games

5. C) They moved to New Orleans

6. C) 5'3"

7. B) Grandmama

8. C) Center

9. B) Kemba Walker

10. B) Rookie of the Year

11. B) A buzzer-beater by Alonzo Mourning

12. B) Kobe Bryant

13. B) Bobcats

14. C) Michael Jordan

15. C) Spectrum Center

NBA PLAYOFF BRACKET

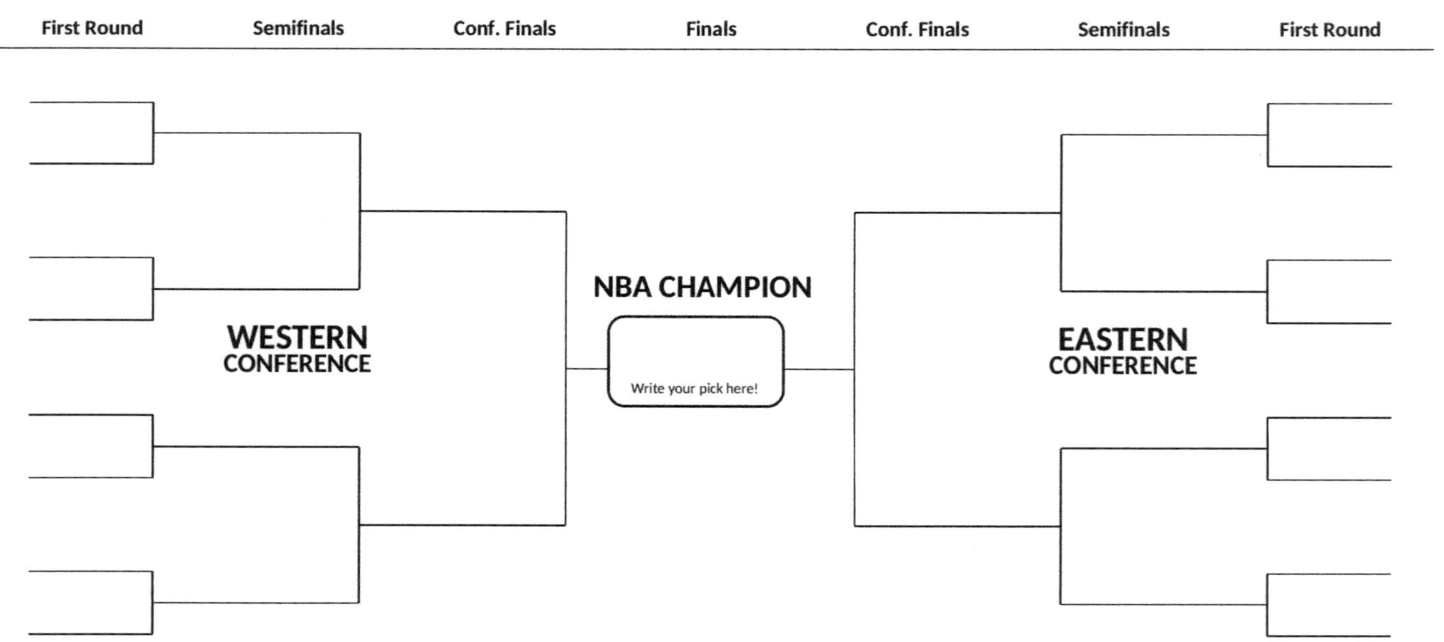

* Fill in your picks and try not to argue with your friends about it!

Part of the Fun Fan Facts: The Unofficial Sports Guide Series

Be the Boss of the Playoffs

You've broken down the matchups. You know which superstar takes over in the fourth quarter. You've seen the bench units that quietly decide series. You've watched the adjustments coaches make when their backs are against the wall.

Now it's time to stop watching and start deciding.

On this page, you are not just a fan. You are the Head Coach drawing up the last play with three seconds left on the clock. You are the GM who built this roster. You are the analyst who saw it all coming.

This is not just filling out a bracket.

This is building your championship run.

Sixteen teams enter the NBA Playoffs. The path is brutal. Best of seven. No shortcuts. No hiding. Every round gets louder, harder, and more personal.

This bracket is your Playoff Control Room.

The Game Plan

1. Survive Round One: Start with the opening round. Which matchup is going seven games? Who has the closer? Who folds under pressure? Make the calls.

2. Feel the Momentum: As you move into the Conference Semifinals and Conference Finals, things change. Role players become heroes. Stars feel the weight. Trust your reads.

3. Own the Finals: Trace your picks all the way to the NBA Finals. When the confetti falls and the trophy is raised, you'll find out who earned it.

House Rules: Circle your boldest upset. That is your official "I knew it" moment.

Choose Your Weapon: Pencil if you want flexibility. Pen if you trust your instincts. Sharpie if you believe in chaos.

Because once the playoffs tip off, there is no rewinding Game 7.

Make your picks. Trust your basketball brain. And let the playoff drama begin.

Fun Facts Wrap-Up

You made it through! You're officially a true superfan!
Now it's time to put your knowledge to the test. Share
these facts with friends and see who really knows their
team best.

Love the series?

Your reviews help other fans discover Fun Fan Facts. If
you enjoyed this book, we'd really appreciate you
sharing your thoughts and leaving a review.

Want more Fun Fan Facts?

Scan the QR code below to visit our site and explore
bonus trivia, challenges, and special extras - including
new teams, future series, and collectible fun as they're
released.

Collect All the Fun Fan Facts Series!

Check off every book you read. See the full set on Amazon. Search "Fun Fan Facts Jake Liam."

World Cup 2026 Edition

☐ Algeria	☐ Scotland	☐ Morocco
☐ France	☐ Brazil	☐ Switzerland
☐ Paraguay	☐ Ivory Coast	☐ Curaçao
☐ Argentina	☐ Senegal	☐ Netherlands
☐ Germany	☐ Canada	☐ Tunisia
☐ Portugal	☐ Japan	☐ Ecuador
☐ Australia	☐ South Africa	☐ New Zealand
☐ Ghana	☐ Cape Verde	☐ United States
☐ Qatar	☐ Jordan	☐ Egypt
☐ Austria	☐ South Korea	☐ Norway
☐ Haiti	☐ Colombia	☐ Uruguay
☐ Saudi Arabia	☐ Mexico	☐ England
☐ Belgium	☐ Spain	☐ Panama
☐ Iran	☐ Croatia	☐ Uzbekistan

World Cup 2026 Group Edition

☐ Group A	☐ Group F	☐ Group K
☐ Group E	☐ Group J	☐ Group D
☐ Group I	☐ Group C	☐ Group H
☐ Group B	☐ Group G	☐ Group L

English Football Edition

- ☐ Arsenal F.C.
- ☐ Aston Villa F.C.
- ☐ Chelsea F.C.
- ☐ Everton F.C.
- ☐ Fulham F.C.
- ☐ Liverpool F.C.
- ☐ Manchester City
- ☐ Manchester United
- ☐ Newcastle United F.C.
- ☐ Tottenham Hotspur
- ☐ West Ham United
- ☐ Wrexham A.F.C.

NBA Edition

- ☐ Atlanta Hawks
- ☐ Boston Celtics
- ☐ Brooklyn Nets
- ☐ Charlotte Hornets
- ☐ Chicago Bulls
- ☐ Cleveland Cavaliers
- ☐ Dallas Mavericks
- ☐ Denver Nuggets
- ☐ Detroit Pistons
- ☐ Golden State Warriors
- ☐ Houston Rockets
- ☐ Indiana Pacers
- ☐ LA Clippers
- ☐ Los Angeles Lakers
- ☐ Memphis Grizzlies
- ☐ Miami Heat
- ☐ Milwaukee Bucks
- ☐ Minnesota Timberwolves
- ☐ New Orleans Pelicans
- ☐ New York Knicks
- ☐ Oklahoma City Thunder
- ☐ Orlando Magic
- ☐ Philadelphia 76ers
- ☐ Phoenix Suns
- ☐ Portland Trail Blazers
- ☐ Sacramento Kings
- ☐ San Antonio Spurs
- ☐ Toronto Raptors
- ☐ Utah Jazz
- ☐ Washington Wizards

About the Author

Jake is a 13-year-old sports fan who loves football, American football, and basketball. He plays soccer as a goalie and dreams of one day playing for West Ham United and helping teach kids to love the game. His passion for sports runs in the family - his dad was a professional baseball player, and his stepdad sparked his love for West Ham. Through the Fun Fan Facts series, he shares the fun and excitement of sports with fans everywhere.